Ninja Foodi Digital Air Fry Oven Cookbook for Family

1000-Day Quick & Easy Delicious Ninja Foodi Digital Air Fry Oven Recipes to Air Fry, Roast, Broil, Bake, Bagel, Toast and Dehydrate

By Kenzi Wood

Table of Contents

Description

For Healthy & Delectable Air fry Oven recipes that taste like a slice of heaven!

Do you want to hear that **satisfying crunch** and experience the burst of **juicy and scrumptious flavors** in your mouth?

Do you desire **delicious sausage casseroles, bacon, toast, egg rolls, baked apples**, among others?

Well, achieving those snacks and meals are with your grasp with this comprehensive cookbook.

Tighten your seat belts because you are about to venture into a world filled with mind-blowing recipes that are easy and affordable. This cookbook contains recipes that can cater to varying numbers of food dieters (Keto, vegan, paleo, among others) with consideration for their diet's dos and don'ts.

The Ninja Foodi Digital Air fry oven cookbook is your ticket to achieving your desired weight effortlessly and joyfully. You will find the following valuable information in the book:

- Thorough Introduction to the Ninja Foodi Digital Air fry Oven
- The components and functions of the Ninja Foodi Digital Air fry Oven.
- Healthy and affordable recipes that will stimulate your taste buds.
- Maintenance, Usage, and Cleaning tips.
- FAQs of the Ninja Foodi Digital Air fry Oven.

Worry less! Cook more! Have an incredible cooking adventure!

Introduction

An adventure of a million years begins from taking a single step. Food lovers typically consider cooking a delightful adventure, and with the Ninja Foodi Digital Air fry oven, every meal is an adventure.

As with every journey, it is crucial to equip yourself with all/most of the required supplies to have a fulfilling and enjoyable one. To maximize the recipes in this cookbook, you need a Ninja Foodi Digital Air fry Oven. Moreover, the unit affords you speed, convenience, dependability, and safety on your cooking "adventure."

With this book and the right equipment, you're ready to take that first step to an unforgettable journey.

Enjoy!

Chapter 1: Ninja Foodi Digital Air fry Oven 101

What is the Ninja Foodi Digital Air Fry Oven?

Is it possible to merge a toaster and convection oven in a single compact unit?

Absolutely!

The Ninja Foodi Digital Air fry Oven's design is a testament to such success. The Ninja Foodi Digital Air fry Oven is an intricately designed cooking appliance that efficiently blends the convection and the toaster oven's unique features.

Here, food is cooked 60% faster than an ordinary oven (a maximum of 20 minutes is enough to prepare most meals). It also produces 75% healthier foods (little to no oil required) regardless of the quantity. The Ninja Foodi Digital Air fry Oven is the key to cooking large while having relatively smaller space thanks to the special flip feature. This feature saves 50% of your counter space when not in use. Unique right?

The Ninja Foodi Digital Air fry Oven can produce about 9 slices of toast, 8 chicken breasts, king-size pizza, and enough fries to feed a family of ten persons. So yeah! It is big enough. Also, it has a noise reduction technology that sets it apart from other brands available

Components and functions of the Ninja Foodi Digital Air fry Oven

The Ninja Foodi Digital Air fry Oven is a multi-functional appliance capable of executing eight different cook programs in isolation or tandem with each other, i.e., multitasking. We have the **Air roast, Bagel, Air fry, Toast, Bake, Air broil, Dehydrate, and keep warm** cooking presets/crisp control. The following are the beautiful and somewhat unbelievable components of the oven unit in more details and their functions:

- **The main unit** is brushed stainless steel, curve edged, and box-like construct inside which all the cooking happens. Within it are the **heating element** and the **fan** that heats air and circulates it, respectively.
- **The Detachable crump tray** is placed below the heating element to collect food crumbs and grease generated while cooking.
- **The Wire rack** placed at the bottom rail position, just above the crumb tray, makes pizza, frozen waffles, bread, among others.
- **The Sheet pan** is responsible for Air roasting protein, veggies, pastries, and bake cake. It places above the wire rack when in use.
- **The Air fry basket** places at the uppermost rail and is used with or without the sheet pan. Your freshly cut or frozen fries and chicken nuggets cook in the basket for that golden brown crisp finish we always love.
- **The control panel** comprises buttons (temperature, time, power, and light), dials (start and pause), temperature/time/darkness indicators, and the brain(otherwise known as the cooking presets that make cooking seamless and enjoyable).
- **The digital crisp control technology** provides you a precision-controlled heat source, airflow mechanism, temperature, 60-second preheat time, and **programmable** cooking presets for the ultimate cooking performance.
- **The flip feature** is used to regain your counter space when not in use by flipping up against the backsplash.

Chapter 2: Usage, maintenance, and cleaning tips

- Before the first use, ensure to remove all packaging labels and tapes. Hand wash all accessories with warm soapy water, rinse and dry thoroughly.

- Study the user manual thoroughly before use to guard against accidents and eventualities. Thankfully, the Ninja Air fry Oven comes with a simple and straightforward user manual.

- Except for the sheet pan and air fryer basket, all accessories are dishwasher safe. Make sure to clean after every use (after it must have completely cooled) to promote durability.

- We recommend you deep clean at least once a week. Firstly, flip the oven to the upright position, remove the back panel, and wipe both the interior and exterior parts with a soft damp cloth soaked with a non-abrasive solution. Never immerse the unit in water.

- The Ninja Air fry Oven is not suitable for outdoor door use. Utilize properly in the comfort of your home.

Chapter 3: FAQs of Ninja Foodi Digital Air fry Oven

- **Is roasting a whole 5-pound chicken possible?** No. However, if the chicken was divided into portions, then it doable.

- **Are steam release and water droplets normal from the oven door?** Yes. This happens with foods that have high moisture content, such as frozen foods.

- **Is the sheet pan compatible with the air fry preset?** Yes. However, the crispy golden result may not be up to par. Endeavor to use the air fry basket instead.

- **Why does the control panel make a sound?** The noise you hear stems from the cooling process of the oven. A fan comes on when the oven becomes very hot to cool it down.

- **What is the warranty policy?** There is a promise of a year warranty and a 60-day money-back guarantee.

Chapter 4: Brunch

Air Fried French Toast

The air-fried french toast is a nice crispy meal with a mouth-watering aroma. An excellent way to start your day

Preparation time: 4 minutes
Cooking time: 6 minutes
Serves: 4

Ingredients To Use:

- 2 slices of sourdough bread
- 1 tbsp. of margarine
- 3 eggs
- 1 tsp. of liquid vanilla

Step-by-Step Directions to Cook It:

1. Preheat the Ninja Foodi Digital Air Fryer Oven by selecting Toast Mode
2. Adjust temperature to 320^{0}F
3. Whisk egg and vanilla together
4. Spread margarine on all sides of the bread.
5. Soak the bread in the egg mixture
6. Arrange on the Ninja Foodi Digital Air Fryer Oven sheet pan
7. Open the door and transfer to the Ninja Foodi Digital Air Fryer Oven
8. Toast for 6 minutes, flipping halfway

Serving suggestions: serve with yogurt and berries

Preparation and Cooking Tips: whisk all the ingredients together

Nutritional value per serving: Calories: 99kcal, Fat: 6g, Carb: 1g, Proteins: 5g

Bell Pepper Egg

Bell pepper egg is a simple and elegant meal that can be eaten with other dishes for breakfast.

Preparation time: 25 minutes
Cooking time: 30 minutes
Serves: 4

Ingredients To Use:

- 4 green bell peppers (cored and seeds removed)
- 8 large eggs
- 1/2 onions, peeled and chopped
- 1 cup Cheddar cheese
- 3 oz. cooked ham, chopped

Step-by-Step Directions to Cook It:

1. Place ham and onion in each bell pepper cup
2. Crack two eggs into each bell pepper and top with cheese
3. Arrange in a muffin tray
4. Preheat the Ninja Foodi Digital Air Fryer Oven by selecting Bake Mode
5. Adjust temperature to 390^{0}F
6. Open the door and transfer to the Ninja Foodi Digital Air Fryer Oven
7. Set time to 15 minutes

Serving suggestions: serve with fruit juice

Preparation and Cooking Tips: cook until pepper is tender

Nutritional value per serving: Calories: 214kcal, Fat: 10g, Carb: 3g, Proteins: 14g

Olives and Kale

Olives and kale are two versatile ingredients that can be used to prepare any meal. The combination of these two creates an excellent breakfast.

Preparation time: 25 minutes
Cooking time: 30 minutes
Serves: 4

Ingredients To Use:

- 1/2 cup black olives, pitted and sliced
- 1 cup chopped kale
- 4 eggs; whisked
- 2 tbsp. grated cheddar
- A pinch of salt and black pepper
- Cooking spray

Step-by-Step Directions to Cook It:

1. Preheat the Ninja Foodi Digital Air Fryer Oven by selecting Bake Mode
2. Adjust temperature to 360^0F
3. Whisk egg and all other ingredients except the cooking spray
4. Pour in the Ninja Foodi Digital Air Fryer Oven sheet pan
5. Bake for 20 minutes
6. Serve and enjoy

Serving suggestions: Enjoy with scrambled egg

Preparation and Cooking Tips: Grease the sheet pan with cooking spray

Nutritional value per serving: Calories: 220kcal, Fat: 10g, Carb: 4g, Proteins: 12g

Wheat and Seed Bread

Wheat and seed bread is another great recipe that can be used in the preparation of bread. It can be enjoyed with any soup of choice.

Preparation time: 70 minutes
Cooking time: 18 minutes
Serves: 4

Ingredients To Use:

- 1/4 cup of pumpkin seeds
- 1/2 cup of flour
- 1/2 cup of wheat flour
- 1 tsp. of yeast
- 3/4 cup of water
- 1 tsp. of salt

Step-by-Step Directions to Cook It:

1. Combine all the dry ingredients
2. Stir in the water and mix until dough is soft, knead for 5 minutes
3. Mold into a ball, cover with plastic wrap and leave to rise for 30 minutes
4. Transfer to a Ninja Foodi Digital Air Fryer Oven sheet pan
5. Preheat the Ninja Foodi Digital Air Fryer Oven by selecting Bake Mode
6. Adjust temperature to 390^{0}F
7. Open the door and transfer to the Ninja Foodi Digital Air Fryer Oven
8. Bake for 18 minutes

Serving suggestions: serve with scrambled egg

Preparation and Cooking Tips: use a lukewarm water

Nutritional value per serving: Calories: 116kcal, Fat: 12g, Carb: 27g, Proteins: 6g

Eggs and Hams Toast Cup

The toast cup is a delicious breakfast meal that's easy to prepare. Be assured that you can consume a healthy breakfast even when in a rush

Preparation time: 5 minutes
Cooking time: 5 minutes
Serves: 2

Ingredients To Use:

- 2 slices of ham
- 2 tbsp. butter
- 2 eggs
- Salt and black pepper to taste

Step-by-Step Directions to Cook It:

1. Preheat the Ninja Foodi Digital Air Fryer Oven by selecting Bake Mode
2. Adjust temperature to 360°F
3. Place a ham slice in each ramekin, crack each egg over ham slices
4. Sprinkle with salt and pepper.
5. Open the door and transfer to Ninja Foodi Digital Air Fryer Oven
6. Bake for 5 minutes
7. Serve and enjoy

Serving suggestions: top with cheddar cheese

Preparation and Cooking Tips: Grease the ramekins with melted butter

Nutritional value per serving: Calories: 201kcal, Fat: 11g, Carb: 5g, Proteins: 9g

Air fried Squash

The air-fried squash is spicy and delicious and an excellent way to start the morning.

Preparation time: 10 minutes
Cooking time: 25 minutes
Serves: 4

Ingredients To Use:

- 2 lbs. yellow Squash, cut into half
- 1 tbsp. olive oil
- 1/4 tsp pepper
- 1 tsp. Italian seasoning
- 1/4 tsp. salt

Step-by-Step Directions to Cook It:

1. Mix all the ingredients in a bowl
2. Pour into the Ninja Foodi Digital Air Fryer Oven sheet pan
3. Preheat the Ninja Foodi Digital Air Fryer Oven by selecting Air Fry Mode
4. Adjust temperature to 390^0F
5. Open the door and transfer to the Ninja Foodi Digital Air Fryer Oven
6. Air fry for 20 minutes
7. Serve and enjoy!

Serving suggestions: serve topped with cheese

Preparation and Cooking Tips: mix all the ingredients well

Nutritional value per serving: Calories: 70kcal, Fat: 4g, Carb: 5g, Proteins: 2g

Croissant with Mushroom and Egg

Croissant with mushroom and egg is an elegant delicacy that is healthy and refreshing. Start your day with this delicacy

Preparation time: 5 minutes
Cooking time: 8 minutes
Serves: 1

Ingredients To Use:

- 1 Croissant
- 4 mushroom, sliced
- 3 slices honey shaved ham
- 4 honey cherry tomato, halved
- 1/2 Rosemary Sprig, diced
- 1/2 cup of shredded cheddar cheese
- 1 Egg

Step-by-Step Directions to Cook It:

1. Grease the Ninja Foodi Digital Air Fryer Oven sheet pan with margarine
2. Arrange the ingredients in layers in the Ninja Foodi Digital Air Fryer Oven sheet pan
3. Sprinkle with salt, black pepper, and rosemary
4. Preheat the Ninja Foodi Digital Air Fryer Oven by selecting Air Fry Mode
5. Adjust temperature to 325⁰F
6. Open the door and transfer to the Ninja Foodi Digital Air Fryer Oven
7. Air fry for 8 minutes, remove croissant after 4 minutes
8. Serve and enjoy!

Serving suggestions: serve with salad and cheesy egg

Preparation and Cooking Tips: arrange the ingredients in layers on the sheet pan

Nutritional value per serving: Calories: 111kcal, Fat: 2g, Carb: 0.3g, Proteins: 6g

Oatmeal Muffins

Oatmeal muffins are a sweet breakfast pastry that can be taken alongside a hot beverage for breakfast.

Preparation time: 5 minutes
Cooking time: 15 minutes
Serves: 4

Ingredients To Use:

- 1/4 cup of oats
- 2 Eggs
- 1 tbsp. raisins
- 1/4 tsp. vanilla essence
- 1/2 cup flour
- 1/2 cup of confectioner's
- 1 block margarine, melted
- Pinch baking powder
- Cooking spray

Step-by-Step Directions to Cook It:

1. Mix all the sugar and margarine until soft. Add egg and vanilla essence and mix
2. In another bowl, combine the remaining ingredients
3. Pour into the Ninja Foodi Digital Air Fryer Oven sheet pan
4. Preheat the Ninja Foodi Digital Air Fryer Oven by selecting bake Mode
5. Adjust temperature to 350^{0}F

6. Open the door and transfer to the Ninja Foodi Digital Air Fryer Oven
7. Bake for 12 minutes
8. Serve and enjoy!

Serving suggestions: serve with a cup of coffee

Preparation and Cooking Tips: spray the sheet pan with cooking spray

Nutritional value per serving: Calories: 108kcal, Fat: 9g, Carb: 1g, Proteins: 6.3g

Parmesan Casserole

The parmesan casserole is another creative way of preparing this dish. It can quickly become your favorite morning dish

Preparation time: 10 minutes
 Cooking time: 20 minutes
Serves: 3

Ingredients To Use:

- 2 tbsp. grated parmesan cheese
- 5 eggs
- 3 tbsp. chunky tomato sauce
- 2 tbsp. heavy cream

Step-by-Step Directions to Cook It:

1. Combine all ingredients in a bowl and mix
2. Pour into the Ninja Foodi Digital Air Fryer Oven sheet pan
3. Preheat the Ninja Foodi Digital Air Fryer Oven by selecting bake Mode
4. Adjust temperature to 325^0F
5. Open the door and transfer to the Ninja Foodi Digital Air Fryer Oven
6. Bake for 20 minutes
7. Serve and enjoy!

Serving suggestions: serve with scrambles eggs

Preparation and Cooking Tips: all ingredients must be thoroughly combined

Nutritional value per serving: Calories: 145kcal, Fat: 14g, Carb: 2g, Proteins: 12g

Air Fried Bacon

Air fried bacon is crispy and can be enjoyed with salad or scrambled eggs. A healthy breakfast treat

Preparation time: 2 minutes
Cooking time: 10 minutes
Serves: 1

Ingredients To Use:

- 4 pieces of bacon

Step-by-Step Directions to Cook It:

1. Place the bacon in the Ninja Foodi Digital Air Fryer Oven air fry basket
2. Preheat the Ninja Foodi Digital Air Fryer Oven by selecting air fry Mode
3. Adjust temperature to 250^0F
4. Open the door and transfer to the Ninja Foodi Digital Air Fryer Oven
5. Air fry for 10 minutes, all until golden brown
6. Serve and enjoy!

Serving suggestions: serve with scrambled egg and salad

Preparation and Cooking Tips: rinse the bacon

Nutritional value per serving: Calories: 165kcal, Fat: 13g, Carb: 0g, Proteins: 13g

Chapter 5: Beef, Pork, and Lamb

Beans and Pork Mix

The beans and pork mix is a delicious and healthy meal that can be eaten for breakfast or lunch.

Preparation time: 10 minutes
 Cooking time: 20 minutes
Serves: 4

Ingredients To Use:

- 1 lb ground pork meat
- 1 cup of canned kidney beans, drained and rinsed
- 1 tsp chili powder
- 1 red onion, chopped
- 1 tbsp. olive oil
- 1/4 tsp ground cumin
- Salt and black pepper to the taste

Step-by-Step Directions to Cook It:

1. Mix all the ingredients in a bowl
2. Pour Ninja Foodi Digital Air Fryer Oven sheet pan
3. Preheat the Ninja Foodi Digital Air Fryer Oven by selecting Bake Mode
4. Adjust temperature to 350^0F
5. Open the door and transfer to the Ninja Foodi Digital Air Fryer Oven
6. Bake for 15 minutes
7. Serve and enjoy!

Serving suggestions: serve with a glass of wine or beverage

Preparation and Cooking Tips: mix all the ingredients

Nutritional value per serving: Calories: 203kcal, Fat: 4g, Carb: 12g, Proteins: 4g

Air Fryer Beef Steak

Air fryer beef steak is crispy on the outside and tender on the inside. It can be served with salad

Preparation time: 5 minutes
Cooking time: 15 minutes
 Serves: 4

Ingredients To Use:

- 2 lbs of ribeye steak
- 1 tbsp. Olive oil
- Pepper and salt

Step-by-Step Directions to Cook It:

1. Season both sides of the meat with pepper and salt, rub with olive oil
2. Place in the Ninja Foodi Digital Air Fryer Oven air fryer basket
3. Preheat the Ninja Foodi Digital Air Fryer Oven by selecting Air fryer Mode
4. Adjust temperature to 350^0F
5. Open the door and transfer to the Ninja Foodi Digital Air Fryer Oven
6. Air fry for 15 minutes, flipping halfway
7. Serve and enjoy!

Serving suggestions: serve with cooked chickpeas

Preparation and Cooking Tips: allow to rest for few minutes before serving

Nutritional value per serving: Calories: 233kcal, Fat: 12g, Carb: 1g, Proteins: 16g

Chili Peppered Lamb Chops

Chili peppered lamb chop is one good spicy dish that will have you craving for more. Perfect for a family dinner

Preparation time: 20 minutes
 Cooking time: 10 minutes
Serves: 6

Ingredients To Use:

- 21 oz. lamb chops
- 1 tsp. cayenne pepper
- 1 tsp. chili pepper
- 1/2 tsp. chili flakes
- 1 tbsp. butter

- 1 tsp. onion powder
- 1 tsp. garlic powder
- 1 tbsp. olive oil
- 1/2 tsp. lime zest

Step-by-Step Directions to Cook It:

1. Add all the ingredients in a bowl, add the lamb and toss to coat
2. Leave to marinate in the fridge for 10 minutes
3. Place in the Ninja Foodi Digital Air Fryer Oven air fryer basket
4. Preheat the Ninja Foodi Digital Air Fryer Oven by selecting Air fry Mode
5. Adjust temperature to 400^{0}F
6. Open the door and transfer to the Ninja Foodi Digital Air Fryer Oven
7. Air fry for 5 minutes
8. Serve and enjoy!

Serving suggestions: serve with salad

Preparation and Cooking Tips: Allow to marinate

Nutritional value per serving: Calories: 227kcal, Fat: 11.6g, Carb: 1g, Proteins: 21g

Pork Stew

It is pork season, and let's get started with a steaming bowl of pork stew. Your day will get better

Preparation time: 35 minutes
Cooking time: 12 minutes
Serves: 4

Ingredients To Use:

- 2 lb. pork, cubed
- 1 tbsp. chopped cilantro
- 1/2 cup beef stock
- 1 eggplant, cubed
- 2 zucchinis, cubed
- 1/2 tsp. smoked paprika
- Salt and black pepper to taste.

Step-by-Step Directions to Cook It:

1. Mix all the ingredients together in a bowl
2. Pour into the Ninja Foodi Digital Air Fryer Oven air fryer sheet pan
3. Preheat the Ninja Foodi Digital Air Fryer Oven by selecting Air Broil Mode
4. Adjust temperature to 370^0F
5. Open the door and transfer to the Ninja Foodi Digital Air Fryer Oven
6. Air broil for 30 minutes, flipping halfway
7. Serve and enjoy!

Serving suggestions: serve with spring onions

Preparation and Cooking Tips: whisk all the ingredients together

Nutritional value per serving: Calories: 241kcal, Fat: 10g, Carb: 11g, Proteins: 17g

Lamb BBQ

Lamb BBQ is the perfect recipe for a neighborhood gathering. It keeps you in a good party mood

Preparation time: 20 minutes
Cooking time: 80 minutes
Serves: 8

Ingredients To Use:

- 4 lbs boneless leg of lamb, cut into chunk
- 2–1/2 tbsp. herb salt
- 2 tbsp. olive oil

Step-by-Step Directions to Cook It:

1. Season both sides of the meat with salt, pepper, and olive oil
2. Place in the Ninja Foodi Digital Air Fryer Oven air fryer basket
3. Preheat the Ninja Foodi Digital Air Fryer Oven by selecting Air fryer Mode
4. Adjust temperature to 390°F
5. Open the door and transfer to the Ninja Foodi Digital Air Fryer Oven
6. Air fry for 20 minutes, flipping halfway
7. Serve and enjoy!

Serving suggestions: serve with any sauce of choice

Preparation and Cooking Tips: leave to marinate for a few minutes

Nutritional value per serving: Calories: 300kcal, Fat: 23g, Carb: 0g, Proteins: 27g

Irish Whiskey Steak

The Irish whisky steak is as delicious as it is spicy. However, the beautiful flavors and aromas are well blended

Preparation time: 4 hours
Cooking time: 20 minutes
Serves: 6

Ingredients To Use:

- 2 lbs sirloin steaks
- 2 tbsp. Irish whiskey
- 1-1/2 tbsp. tamari sauce
- 2 tbsp. olive oil
- 1/3 tsp cayenne pepper
- 2 garlic cloves, minced
- 1/3 tsp ground ginger
- Fine sea salt, to taste

Step-by-Step Directions to Cook It:

1. Add all the ingredients in a bowl, except the steak and the oil.
2. Pour in a Ziploc bag and leave to marinate for a few hours. Drizzle the meat with oil
3. Place in the Ninja Foodi Digital Air Fryer Oven air fryer basket
4. Preheat the Ninja Foodi Digital Air Fryer Oven by selecting Air roast Mode
5. Adjust temperature to 395°F
6. Open the door and transfer to the Ninja Foodi Digital Air Fryer Oven
7. Air roast for 22 minutes, flipping halfway through.
8. Serve and enjoy!

Serving suggestions: serve with vegetable salad and sauce

Preparation and Cooking Tips: leave to marinate for a long time to get a juicy meat

Nutritional value per serving: Calories: 260kcal, Fat: 12g, Carb: 2g, Proteins: 27g

Bacon-Wrapped Pork

Bacon-wrapped pork is crispy on the outside, tender and juicy on the inside. The perfect family lunch

Preparation time: 15 minutes
Cooking time: 14 minutes
Serves: 6

Ingredients To Use:

- 1 lb pork brisket, cut into medium size
- 1 tbsp. apple cider vinegar
- 6 slice of bacon
- 1 tsp turmeric powder
- 1 tsp salt
- 1/2 tsp red pepper
- 1 tsp olive oil

Step-by-Step Directions to Cook It:

1. Add all ingredients in a bowl except the bacon, toss to coat.
2. Leave to marinate for a few minutes, wrap bacon around the pork chops.
3. Secure with toothpicks
4. Place in the Ninja Foodi Digital Air Fryer Oven air fryer basket
5. Preheat the Ninja Foodi Digital Air Fryer Oven by selecting Air fryer Mode
6. Adjust temperature to 370^0F
7. Open the door and transfer to the Ninja Foodi Digital Air Fryer Oven
8. Air fry for 8 minutes, flip and cook for an additional 6 minutes
9. Serve and enjoy!

Serving suggestions: serve with sauce

Preparation and Cooking Tips: secure bacon and pork with a toothpick

Nutritional value per serving: Calories: 239kcal, Fat: 11g, Carb: 2.8g, Proteins: 26g

Skewered Sausage

Skewered sausage is full of flavors and has great taste. It can be enjoyed as an outdoor gathering meal.

Preparation time: 20 minutes
Cooking time: 20 minutes
Serves: 4

Ingredients To Use:

- 1 lb. smoked beef sausage, sliced
- 2 tbsps. Worcestershire sauce
- 1 tbsp. mustard
- 2 bell peppers, sliced
- 1 tbsp. olive oil
- Salt and ground black pepper, to taste

Step-by-Step Directions to Cook It:

1. Add all the ingredients in a bowl and toss to coat, thread on the skewer
2. Place in the Ninja Foodi Digital Air Fryer Oven air fryer basket
3. Preheat the Ninja Foodi Digital Air Fryer Oven by selecting Air Fryer Mode
4. Adjust temperature to 360°F
5. Open the door and transfer to the Ninja Foodi Digital Air Fryer Oven
6. Air fry for 10 minutes, flipping halfway
7. Serve and enjoy!

Serving suggestions: serve with sauce

Preparation and Cooking Tips: Arrange bell pepper and sausage on the skewer

Nutritional value per serving: Calories: 321kcal, Fat: 21g, Carb: 5g, Proteins: 16g

Fragrant Pork Tenderloins

This dish's aroma is one to die for; let's not forget about the delicious taste. Treat yourself to a pleasant and sumptuous dinner.

Preparation time: 20 minutes
Cooking time: 15 minutes
Serves: 3

Ingredients To Use:

- 1 lb pork tenderloin
- 1 tsp. sage
- 1 tbsp. apple cider vinegar
- 1/2 tsp ground cinnamon
- 1 tsp garlic powder

- 3 tbsp. butter
- 1/2 tsp saffron
- 1 tsp onion powder
- 1 garlic clove, crushed

Step-by-Step Directions to Cook It:

1. Add all the ingredients to a bowl, toss to coat.
2. Leave to marinate for a few minutes
3. Place in the Ninja Foodi Digital Air Fryer Oven air fryer basket
4. Preheat the Ninja Foodi Digital Air Fryer Oven by selecting Air fry Mode
5. Adjust temperature to 325^0F
6. Open the door and transfer to the Ninja Foodi Digital Air Fryer Oven
7. Air fry for 15 minutes.
8. Serve and enjoy!

Serving suggestions: Enjoy with salad

Preparation and Cooking Tips: allow to marinate for a few hours

Nutritional value per serving: Calories: 297kcal, Fat: 12g, Carb: 2g, Proteins: 27g

Spicy Paprika Steak

The recipe is one to remember for lovers of spicy food. This recipe will more than meet your expectations, enjoy!

Preparation time: 20 minutes
Cooking time: 20 minutes
Serves: 2

Ingredients To Use:

- 2 beef steaks
- 1/2 Ancho chili pepper, soaked in hot water before using
- 2 tsp. smoked paprika
- 1-1/2 tbsp. olive oil
- 1 tbsp. brandy
- 1tsp ground allspice
- Salt to taste
- 3 cloves garlic, sliced

Step-by-Step Directions to Cook It:

1. Season both sides of the meat with salt, allspice, and paprika.
2. Place in the Ninja Foodi Digital Air Fryer Oven air fryer sheet pan
3. Drizzle with oil, spread garlic and ancho chili pepper on top
4. Preheat the Ninja Foodi Digital Air Fryer Oven by selecting Air fryer Mode
5. Adjust temperature to 385°F
6. Open the door and transfer to the Ninja Foodi Digital Air Fryer Oven
7. Air fry for 15 minutes, flipping halfway
8. Serve and enjoy!

Serving suggestions: serve with sliced vegetables

Preparation and Cooking Tips: leave to marinate for some minutes

Nutritional value per serving: Calories: 300kcal, Fat: 14g, Carb: 1g, Proteins: 23g

Chapter 6: Fish ad Seafood

Air Fried Salmon

This crispy bit of heaven is the best for a night out. It can be enjoyed with ready-made sauce.

Preparation time: 12 minutes
Cooking time: 5 minutes
Serves: 4

Ingredients To Use:

- 4 salmon fillets
- 6 tbsp. Soy Sauce
- 1 tbsp. brown sugar
- 1/2 tbsp. Minced Garlic
- 1 Green onion finely chopped
- 1/4 cup Dijon Mustard

Step-by-Step Directions to Cook It:

1. Add the fish and other ingredients to a bowl, toss to coat.
2. Leave to marinate in the fridge for 30 minutes
3. Place in the Ninja Foodi Digital Air Fryer Oven air fryer basket
4. Preheat the Ninja Foodi Digital Air Fryer Oven by selecting Air fry Mode
5. Adjust temperature to 390⁰F
6. Open the door and transfer to the Ninja Foodi Digital Air Fryer Oven

7. Air fry for 12 minutes, flipping halfway.
8. Serve and enjoy!

Serving suggestions: serve with chopped green onion and lemon wedges

Preparation and Cooking Tips: leave to marinate for a few minutes

Nutritional value per serving: Calories: 267kcal, Fat: 9g, Carb: 2g, Proteins: 18g

Lobster Tail

Lobster tail is an exotic recipe that's excellent for lunch or dinner. Also, seafood is always healthy for consumption.

Preparation time: 5 minutes
Cooking time: 8 minutes
Serves: 2

Ingredients To Use:

- 2 (6 oz.) lobster tails,
- 1 tsp lemon juice
- 2 tbsp. unsalted butter melted
- 1 tsp chopped chives
- 1 tsp salt
- 1 tbsp. minced garlic

Step-by-Step Directions to Cook It:

1. Add all the ingredients together in a bowl
2. Arrange the lobster tail in the Ninja Foodi Air Fryer Oven sheet pan
3. Spread butter mixture over the lobster meat.
4. Preheat the Ninja Foodi Air Fryer Oven by selecting air fry mode
5. Adjust temperature to 390^{0}F
6. Open the door and transfer to the Ninja Foodi Digital Air Fryer Oven
7. Air fry for 10 minutes.
8. Serve and enjoy!

Serving suggestions: Enjoy with any side dish of choice

Preparation and Cooking Tips: remove the meat and place on top of the shell

Nutritional value per serving: Calories: 120kcal, Fat: 12g, Carb: 2g, Proteins: 1g

Baked Shrimp Scampi

Baked Shrimp Scambi is flavourful and delicious, perfect for a romantic dinner. Enjoy with a side dish and a glass of wine

Preparation time: 10 minutes
Cooking time: 10 minutes
Serves: 4

Ingredients To Use:

- 1 lb large shrimp
- 1 tbsp. minced garlic
- 1/2 tsp onion powder
- 1/4 cup white wine
- 8 tbsp. butter, melted
- 1/4 tsp cayenne pepper
- 1/4 tsp paprika
- 1/2 tsp salt
- 3/4 cup bread crumbs

Step-by-Step Directions to Cook It:

1. In a casserole pan, add all the ingredients. Add the shrimp and mix
2. Preheat the Ninja Foodi Air Fryer Oven by selecting bake mode
3. Adjust temperature to 350^{0}F
4. Open the door and transfer to the Ninja Foodi Digital Air Fryer Oven
5. Bake for 10 minutes.
6. Serve and enjoy

Serving suggestions: serve with lemon wedges

Preparation and Cooking Tips: use 2 tbsp. of garlic for extra garlic flavor

Nutritional value per serving: Calories: 322kcal, Fat: 21g, Carb: 15g, Proteins: 27g

Coconut Crusted Shrimps

Seafood is always a good way to enjoy your evening dinner. The flavor is so coconutty.

Preparation time: 15 minutes
Cooking time: 40 minutes
Serves: 3

Ingredients To Use:

- 1 lb large shrimp, peeled and deveined
- 1/4 cup of coconut milk
- 1/2 cup panko breadcrumbs
- 1/2 cup sweetened coconut, shredded
- Salt and black pepper, to taste

Step-by-Step Directions to Cook It:

1. Place coconut milk in a bowl.
2. add coconut, breadcrumbs, salt, and pepper in another bowl
3. Dip each shrimp in the coconut milk, then in the coconut mixture
4. Arrange the shrimp in the Ninja Foodie Air Fryer Oven air fry basket
5. Preheat the Ninja Foodi Air Fryer Oven by selecting Air fry mode
6. Adjust temperature to 350^{0}F
7. Open the door and transfer to the Ninja Foodi Digital Air Fryer Oven
8. Air fry for 10 minutes

Serving suggestions: serve with avocado salsa

Preparation and Cooking Tips: mix all ingredients together.

Nutritional value per serving: Calories: 307kcal, Fat: 13g, Carb: 10g, Proteins: 21g

Rice Crusted Coconut Shrimp

This dish is one to remember; the flavor is simply incredible and can be prepared with simple steps

Preparation time: 20 minutes
Cooking time: 20 minutes
Serves: 3

Ingredients To Use:

- 1 lb shrimp, peeled and deveined
- 2 tbsp. olive oil
- 3 tbsp. rice flour
- 2 tbsp. olive oil
- 1 tsp. powdered sugar
- Salt and black pepper, to taste

Step-by-Step Directions to Cook It:

1. Add all the ingredients together in a bowl, stir in the shrimps
2. Pour in the Ninja Foodi Digital Air Fryer Oven air fryer basket
3. Preheat the Ninja Foodi Digital Air Fryer Oven by selecting Air fry Mode
4. Adjust temperature to 325^{0}F
5. Open the door and transfer to the Ninja Foodi Digital Air Fryer Oven
6. Air fry for 10 minutes, flipping halfway.

Serving suggestions: serve with marinara sauce

Preparation and Cooking Tips: mix all the ingredients.

Nutritional value per serving: Calories: 299kcal, Fat: 12g, Carb: 11g, Proteins: 25g

Prawn Burgers

Prawns are delicious and tasty; moreover, air frying creates juicy and crispy prawns.

Preparation time: 20 minutes
Cooking time: 6 minutes
Serves: 2

Ingredients To Use:

- 1/2 cup prawns, peeled, deveined, and finely chopped
- 3 tbsp. onion, finely chopped
- 1/2 tsp. garlic, minced
- 1/2 tsp. red chili powder
- 1/2 tsp. ground cumin
- 1/2 tsp ginger, minced
- 1/2 cup breadcrumbs
- 1/4 tsp. ground turmeric
- Salt and ground black pepper to taste

Step-by-Step Directions to Cook It:

1. Preheat the Ninja Foodi Air fryer Oven by selecting air fry mode
2. Adjust temperature to 390^{0}F
3. Mix all the ingredients in a bowl, form into small patties
4. Pour in the Ninja Foodi Air Fryer Oven air fryer basket
5. Open the door and transfer to the Ninja Foodi Digital Air Fryer Oven
6. Air fry for 6 minutes.

Serving suggestions: serve with fresh baby greens

Preparation and Cooking Tips: mix ingredients together

Nutritional value per serving: Calories: 240kcal, Fat: 2.7g, Carb: 17g, Proteins: 18g

Caspian Cod

Caspian cod is a simple and elegant meal that can be prepared for lunch or dinner.

Preparation time: 12 minutes
Cooking time: 10 minutes
Serves: 5

Ingredients To Use:

- 1 lb. Cod
- 2 eggs
- 3 tbsp. Milk
- 2 cups Breadcrumbs
- 1 cup Almond flour

Step-by-Step Directions to Cook It:

1. Preheat the Ninja Foodi Air Fryer Oven by selecting air fry mode
2. Adjust temperature to 390°F
3. Mix egg and milk in a bowl; in another bowl, add breadcrumbs.
4. In a third, add the almond flour.
5. Dip the fillet in each bowl and transfer to the Ninja Foodi Air Fryer Oven air fry basket
6. Open the door and transfer to the Ninja Foodi Digital Air Fryer Oven
7. Air fry for 12 minutes

Serving suggestions: serve with sliced avocado pear

Preparation and Cooking Tips: mix all ingredients

Nutritional value per serving: Calories: 271kcal, Fat: 8g, Carb: 15g, Proteins: 19g

Crispy Salmon

Marinating this recipe brings out the flavor. The result of this recipe is a nice and juicy salmon

Preparation time: 1 hour 20 minutes
Cooking time: 20 minutes
Serves: 2

Ingredients To Use:

- 2 salmon steaks
- Zest from 1 lemon
- 1 tbsp. fresh lemon juice
- 1/2 tsp smoked cayenne pepper
- Salt and black pepper to taste
- 1 tsp garlic, minced
- 1/2 tsp dried dill

Step-by-Step Directions to Cook It:

1. Mix all the ingredients in a bowl, add the fish and leave to marinate for 1 hour
2. Pour in the Ninja Foodi Air Fryer Oven air fryer basket
3. Preheat the Ninja Foodi Air fryer Oven by selecting air fry mode
4. Adjust temperature to 370^0F
5. Open the door and transfer to the Ninja Foodi Digital Air Fryer Oven
6. Air fry for 12 minutes. Meanwhile, cook the marinade on medium heat until sauce thickens

Serving suggestions: Serve with the marinade

Preparation and Cooking Tips: leave to marinate for at least 1 hour

Nutritional value per serving: Calories: 346kcal, Fat: 15g, Carb: 4g, Proteins: 27g

Cod with Avocado Mayo Sauce

The crispy cod is delicious but, when coupled with the avocado mayo sauce, simply creates a unique taste.

Preparation time: 20 minutes
Cooking time: 20 minutes
Serves: 2

Ingredients To Use:

- 2 cod fish fillets
- 1 egg
- 2tsps olive oil
- 1/2 avocado, peeled, pitted, and mashed
- 1/2 tsp. yellow mustard
- 1 tsp. lemon juice
- 1 garlic clove, minced
- 1 tbsp. mayonnaise
- 3 tbsp. sour cream
- 1/4 tsp. black pepper
- 1/4 tsp. salt
- 1/4 tsp hot pepper sauce

Step-by-Step Directions to Cook It:

1. Preheat the Ninja Foodi Air Fryer Oven by selecting air fry mode
2. Adjust temperature to 360°F
3. Mix egg, olive oil, and salt in a bowl. Add the fish and toss to coat.
4. Transfer to the Ninja Foodi Air Fryer Oven air fry basket
5. Open the door and transfer to the Ninja Foodi Digital Air Fryer Oven
6. Air fry for 12 minutes
7. Meanwhile, mix the remaining ingredients in a bowl and refrigerate.

Serving suggestions: serve with avocado sauce

Preparation and Cooking Tips: pat dry the fish

Nutritional value per serving: Calories: 312kcal, Fat: 21g, Carb:8g, Proteins: 21g

Garlic Parmesan Shrimp

The garlic parmesan shrimps have it all, from flavor to aroma to taste.

Preparation time: 20 minutes
Cooking time: 10 minutes
Serves: 2

Ingredients To Use:

- 1 lb shrimp, deveined and peeled
- 1/2 cup parmesan cheese, grated
- 1 tbsp. olive oil
- Salt and black pepper to taste
- 1tbsp lemon juice
- 6 garlic cloves, diced

Step-by-Step Directions to Cook It:

1. Drizzle shrimps with oil, lemon juice, garlic, and crack pepper.
2. Leave to marinate for at least 3 hours, stir in the cheese
3. Pour in the Ninja Foodi Air Fryer Oven sheet pan
4. Preheat the Ninja Foodi Air fryer Oven by selecting air fry mode
5. Adjust temperature to 350^{0}F
6. Open the door and transfer to the Ninja Foodi Digital Air Fryer Oven
7. Air fry for 12 minutes.

Serving suggestions: serve garnish with parsley

Preparation and Cooking Tips: leave to marinate for at least 3 hours

Nutritional value per serving: Calories: 302kcal, Fat: 16g, Carb: 19g, Proteins: 10g

Chapter 7: Chicken and Poultry

Maple Chicken Thigh

The maple chicken thigh is juicy and tender meat that gives this sweet and savory taste.

Preparation time: 10 minutes
Cooking time: 30 minutes
 Serves: 4

Ingredients To Use:

- 4 large chicken thighs, bone-in
- 1 clove minced garlic
- 1/2 tsp. dried marjoram
- 2 tbsp. French mustard
- 2 tbsp. Dijon mustard
- 2 tbsp. maple syrup

Step-by-Step Directions to Cook It:

1. Preheat the Ninja Foodi Air Fryer Oven by selecting air fry mode
2. Adjust temperature to 370^0F
3. Mix chicken and all the ingredients in a bowl.
4. Pour into the Ninja Foodi Air Fryer Oven sheet pan
5. Open the door and transfer to the Ninja Foodi Digital Air Fryer Oven
6. Air fry for 30 minutes

Serving suggestions: Serve with the sauce

Preparation and Cooking Tips: allow to marinate for a few minutes

Nutritional value per serving: Calories: 201kcal, Fat: 11g, Carb: 5g, Proteins: 23g

Air Fried Turkey Wings

The air-fried turkey wings are so yummy, prepare for a little get together party.
Space for Image
Preparation time: 10 minutes
Cooking time: 26 minutes
 Serves: 4

Ingredients To Use:

- 2 lbs turkey wings
- 3tbsp. olive oil
- 4 tbsp. chicken rub

Step-by-Step Directions to Cook It:

1. Preheat the Ninja Foodi Air Fryer Oven by selecting air fry mode
2. Adjust temperature to 380^0F
3. Mix turkey and all the ingredients in a bowl.
4. Pour into the Ninja Foodi Air Fryer Oven sheet pan
5. Open the door and transfer to the Ninja Foodi Digital Air Fryer Oven
6. Air fry for 26 minutes, flip once

Serving suggestions: serve with ketchup

Preparation and Cooking Tips: leave to marinate for a few minutes

Nutritional value per serving: Calories: 204kcal, Fat: 11g, Carb: 2g, Proteins: 12g

Duck Roll

The duck roll can be a good side dish or main dish, depending on the occasion. However, it is best enjoyed with the sauce

Preparation time: 20 minutes
Cooking time: 40 minutes
Serves: 3

Ingredients To Use:

- 1 lb. duck breast fillet, each cut into 2 pieces
- 1 garlic clove, crushed
- 1 small red onion, chopped
- 1-1/2 tsp. ground cumin
- 1 tsp. ground cinnamon
- 1/2 tsp. red chili powder
- 3 tbsp. chopped parsley
- Salt, to taste
- 2 tbsp. olive oil

Step-by-Step Directions to Cook It:

1. Preheat the Ninja Foodi Air Fryer Oven by selecting air fry mode
2. Adjust temperature to 355°F
3. Mix all the ingredients in a bowl, coat the meat in the mixture
4. Roll each duck and transfer to the Ninja Foodi Air Fryer Oven air fry basket
5. Open the door and transfer to the Ninja Foodi Digital Air Fryer Oven
6. Air fry for 40 minutes, flip once

Serving suggestions: serve with sauce

Preparation and Cooking Tips: mix all the spices

Nutritional value per serving: Calories: 231kcal, Fat: 6g, Carb: 3g, Proteins: 27g

Spicy Crusted Chicken

Spicy crusted chicken is so delicious it will leave your tongue wanting more.

Preparation time: 10 minutes
Cooking time: 40 minutes
Serves: 6

Ingredients To Use:

- 1 lb chicken cut into pieces
- 6 eggs, beaten
- 4 tsp. thyme
- 6 tsp. oregano
- 6 tsp. parsley
- 4 tsp. paprika
- Salt and freshly ground black pepper, to taste

Step-by-Step Directions to Cook It:

1. Preheat the Ninja Foodi Air Fryer Oven by selecting air fry mode
2. Adjust temperature to 355^0F
3. Whisk egg in a bowl, mix all the other ingredients except chicken in another bowl
4. Dip the chicken in the egg and then in the dry mixture
5. Transfer to the Ninja Foodi Air Fryer Oven air fry basket
6. Open the door and transfer to the Ninja Foodi Digital Air Fryer Oven
7. Air fry for 20 minutes, flip once

Serving suggestions: serve garnish with cilantro

Preparation and Cooking Tips: coat the chicken well

Nutritional value per serving: Calories: 218kcal, Fat: 9g, Carb: 2g, Proteins: 27g

Herbed Duck Leg

Herbed Duck leg includes the combination of different spices that are well blended in flavor and aromas.

Preparation time: 10 minutes
Cooking time: 30 minutes
 Serves: 2

Ingredients To Use:

- 2 duck legs
- 1/2 tbsp. chopped fresh thyme
- 1 garlic clove, minced
- 1/2 tbsp. chopped fresh parsley
- 1 tsp. five-spice powder
- Salt and black pepper, as required

Step-by-Step Directions to Cook It:

1. Preheat the Ninja Foodi Air Fryer Oven by selecting air fry mode
2. Adjust temperature to 340^0F
3. Mix all the mixture, add the duck leg. Toss to coat
4. Transfer to the Ninja Foodi Air Fryer Oven air fry basket
5. Open the door and transfer to the Ninja Foodi Digital Air Fryer Oven
6. Air fry for 25 minutes, flipping halfway through

Serving suggestions: serve garnished with parsley

Preparation and Cooking Tips: leave to marinate for a few minutes

Nutritional value per serving: Calories: 132kcal, Fat: 4g, Carb: 1g, Proteins: 25g

Butter Duck Breast

Butter duck breast is creamy and juicy. The tender meat just melts in your mouth as you chew.

Preparation time: 15 minutes
Cooking time: 22 minutes
Serves: 4

Ingredients To Use:

- 2 oz. duck breast
- 3 tbsp. unsalted butter, melted
- 1/2 tsp. dried thyme
- 1/4 tsp. star anise powder
- Salt and ground black pepper to taste

Step-by-Step Directions to Cook It:

1. Preheat the Ninja Foodi Air Fryer Oven by selecting air fry mode
2. Adjust temperature to 390^0F
3. Mix all the ingredients in a bowl, add the duck breast and toss to coat
4. Transfer to the Ninja Foodi Air Fryer Oven air fry basket
5. Open the door and transfer to the Ninja Foodi Digital Air Fryer Oven
6. Air fry for 15 minutes, flipping halfway through

Serving suggestions: serve with baked potatoes

Preparation and Cooking Tips: leave to marinate for few minutes

Nutritional value per serving: Calories: 300kcal, Fat: 13g, Carb: 1g, Proteins: 26g

Oven-Baked Chicken Thigh

Oven-baked chicken thigh is a meal to enjoy a romantic evening with your partner.

Preparation time: 10 minutes
Cooking time: 26 minutes
Serves: 4

Ingredients To Use:

- 4 chicken thigh, bone-in
- 4 tbsp. chicken rub
- 3 tbsp. olive oil

Step-by-Step Directions to Cook It:

1. Preheat the Ninja Foodi Air Fryer Oven by selecting Bake mode
2. Adjust temperature to 380^{0}F
3. Mix chicken and all the ingredients in a bowl.
4. Pour into the Ninja Foodi Air Fryer Oven sheet pan
5. Open the door and transfer to the Ninja Foodi Digital Air Fryer Oven
6. Bake for 20 minutes, flip once

Serving suggestions: serve with yogurt and berries

Preparation and Cooking Tips: whisk all the ingredients

Nutritional value per serving: Calories: 201kcal, Fat: 11g, Carb: 3g, Proteins: 16g

Lemon Pepper Turkey

Lemon Pepper turkey has this tangy, delicious taste that will leave you wanting more.

Preparation time: 10 minutes
Cooking time: 45 minutes
Serves: 6

Ingredients To Use:

- 3 lbs. turkey breast
- 1 tbsp. Worcestershire sauce
- 2 tbsp. oil
- 1 tsp. lemon pepper
- 1/2 tsp. salt

Step-by-Step Directions to Cook It:

1. Preheat the Ninja Foodi Air Fryer Oven by selecting air fry mode
2. Adjust temperature to 375^0F
3. Mix turkey and all the ingredients in a bowl.
4. Pour into the Ninja Foodi Air Fryer Oven air fryer basket
5. Open the door and transfer to the Ninja Foodi Digital Air Fryer Oven
6. Air fry for 45 minutes, flip once

Serving suggestions: serve with gravy

Preparation and Cooking Tips: leave to marinate for few minutes

Nutritional value per serving: Calories: 321kcal, Fat: 3g, Carb: 6g, Proteins: 23g

Chicken Meatballs

Meatballs are known for the delicious taste they bring to any meal. Serve with tomato sauce as a main meal

Preparation time: 10 minutes
Cooking time: 10 minutes
Serves: 4

Ingredients To Use:

- 1 lb. ground chicken
- 1/3 cup panko breadcrumbs
- 2 tsp. chives
- 1/2 tsp. garlic powder
- 1 tsp. thyme
- 1 egg
- 1 tsp. salt

Step-by-Step Directions to Cook It:

1. Mix all the ingredients together, form into small balls
2. Preheat the Ninja Foodi Air Fryer Oven by selecting air fry mode
3. Adjust temperature to 355^0F
4. Transfer meatball to the Ninja Foodi Air Fryer Oven air fryer basket
5. Open the door and transfer to the Ninja Foodi Digital Air Fryer Oven
6. Air fry for 10 minutes

Serving suggestions: serve with noodles and tomato sauce

Preparation and Cooking Tips: use ice-cream scooper to form the balls

Nutritional value per serving: Calories: 321kcal, Fat: 3g, Carb: 18g, Proteins: 24g

Ranch Chicken Wings

This recipe is tasty with it crispy appearance and tasty flavours. They are all present in this dish.

Preparation time: 10 minutes
Cooking time: 10 minutes
 Serves: 3

Ingredients To Use:

- 6 chicken wings, bone-in
- 1/4 cup almond meal
- 1 tbsp. Ranch seasoning mix
- 1/4 cup flaxseed
- 6 tbsp. grated parmesan cheese
- 2 tbsp. butter, melted
- 2 tbsp. oyster sauce

Step-by-Step Directions to Cook It:

1. Mix all the ingredients, pour into a resealable bag.
2. Add the chicken and leave to marinate for 30 minutes
3. Preheat the Ninja Foodi Air Fryer Oven by selecting air fry mode
4. Adjust temperature to 370^0F
5. Transfer the meat to the Ninja Foodi Air Fryer Oven air fryer basket
6. Open the door and transfer to the Ninja Foodi Digital Air Fryer Oven
7. Air fry for 11 minutes, turn and cook for additional 11 minutes

Serving Suggestion: Serve with your favorite dipping sauce

Preparation and Cooking Tip: toss to coat the meat, allow to marinate

Nutritional value per serving: Calories: 285kcal, Fat: 11g, Carb: 3g, Proteins: 16g

Chapter 8: Vegan and Vegetarian Recipes

Carrots and Beets

The mixture of carrots and beets result in a fabulous meal. It is also excellent for summer weight loss.

Preparation time: 10 minutes
Cooking time: 21 minutes
Serves: 5

Ingredients To Use:

- 2 tbsp of olive oil
- 1 pound beets
- 1 tbsp of chives
- Black pepper and salt
- 1 pound of baby carrot

Step-by-Step Directions to Cook It:

1. Mix pepper, beets, chives, carrot, and olive oil in a bowl.
2. Place the mixture in the Ninja Foodi Air Fryer Oven basket.
3. Set the Ninja Foodi Air Fryer Oven to air crisp
4. Cook for 20 minutes at 390°F
5. Serve immediately.

Serving Suggestions: serve with mayonnaise or ketchup

Preparation & Cooking Tips: Peel and cut beets into cubes. Peel the carrots

Nutritional value per serving: Calories: 151kcal, Fat: 6g, Carb: 8g, Proteins: 4g

Radishes Mint

Minty radish is a great meal that stands out due to its captivating taste and irresistible aroma

Preparation time: 10 minutes
Cooking time: 16 minutes
Serves: 5

Ingredients To Use:

- 2 tbsp of balsamic vinegar
- 1 pond of radishes
- 2 tbsp of olive oil
- Black pepper and salt
- 2 tbsp of mint

Step-by-Step Directions to Cook It:

1. Preheat the Ninja Foodi Digital Air Fryer Oven by selecting air fry mode
2. Mix radishes, mint, olive oil, balsamic vinegar, salt, and pepper in a bowl.
3. Place the ingredients in the Ninja Foodi Air Fryer Oven basket.
4. Cook the radish mix on air-fry mode for 16 minutes at 380^0F
5. Serve the radishes immediately.

Serving Suggestions: Serve with mint chutney

Preparation & Cooking Tips: chop the mint. Cut the radish into half

Nutritional value per serving: Calories: 171kcal, Fat: 5g, Carb: 8g, Proteins: 5.2g

Walnuts with Carrots Salad

Walnut and carrots salad is a great breakfast meal; try it out on your Ninja Foodi Air Fryer Oven

Preparation time: 10 minutes
Cooking time: 16 minutes
Serves: 3

Ingredients To Use:

- 1 cup of chicken stock
- 4 carrots
- 1 tbsp of olive oil
- Black pepper and salt
- 1/2 cup of walnuts
- 3 tbsp of balsamic vinegar

Step-by-Step Directions to Cook It:

1. Preheat the Ninja Foodi Digital Air Fryer Oven by selecting air fry mode
2. Mix chicken stock, carrots, olive oil, walnut, salt, balsamic vinegar, and pepper.
3. Transfer the mixture to the Ninja Foodi Air Fryer Oven pan
4. Cook for 16 minutes at 350°F.
5. Serve immediately

Serving Suggestions: serve with mayonnaise

Preparation & Cooking Tips: shred the carrots and slice the walnuts

Nutritional value per serving: Calories: 121kcal, Fat: 5g, Carb: 6g, Proteins: 2g

Kale with Eggplant Chili

Eggplant and kale make a great meal; you can't go wrong with this meal.

Preparation time: 10 minutes
Cooking time: 16 minutes
Serves: 5

Ingredients To Use:

- 1/2 tsp of chili powder
- 1 lime juice
- 3 tbsp of olive oil
- Black pepper and salt
- 1/2 cup of chicken stock
- 1 cup of kale
- 1 pound of eggplant

Step-by-Step Directions to Cook It:

1. Preheat the Ninja Foodi Digital Air Fryer Oven by selecting air fry mode
2. Pour the oil and the eggplant into the air fryer pan and heat for two minutes.
3. Add kale and the remaining ingredients
4. Cook for 14 minutes at 360°F
5. Serve immediately.

Serving Suggestions: serve with mayonnaise

Preparation & Cooking Tips: cut eggplant into cubes

Nutritional value per serving: Calories: 111kcal, Fat: 3.3g, Carb: 5.1g, Proteins: 2g

Cauliflower with Lime Broccoli

Having a meal with a sweet taste is a priority. A combination of cauliflower and broccoli gives a crunchy meal. Lime also provide the vegetables with lasting flavor

Preparation time: 11 minutes
Cooking time: 16 minutes
Serves: 5

Ingredients To Use:

- 1 tbsp of avocado oil
- 2 tsp of minced garlic
- 2 cups of broccoli florets
- 2 tbsp of lime juice
- 1/3 cup of tomato sauce
- 1 cup of cauliflower florets
- 1 tbsp of chives
- 2 tsp of ginger

Step-by-Step Directions to Cook It:

1. Preheat the Ninja Foodi Digital Air Fryer Oven by selecting air fry mode
2. Add the oil to the Air Fryer Oven pan
3. Add the ginger, garlic, and heat for 2 minutes
4. Add the cauliflower, broccoli, and remaining ingredients.
5. Cook for 14 minutes at 360°F
6. Serve immediately

Serving Suggestions: serve with any juice

Preparation & Cooking Tips: chop the chives and grate the garlic

Nutritional value per serving: Calories: 120kcal, Fat: 2g, Carb: 5g, Proteins: 7g

Spinach with Zucchinis

These vegetables make a fantastic meal. This meal can be prepared for dinner dates or on a special occasion.

Preparation time: 10 minutes
Cooking time: 16 minutes
Serves: 4

Ingredients To Use:

- 1 tbsp of avocado oil
- 2 zucchinis
- 1/2 tsp of chili powder
- Black pepper and salt
- 1 chopped red onion
- 1 pound of baby spinach
- 1 tbsp of sweet paprika
- 1/2 cup of tomato sauce
- 1/2 tsp of garlic powder

Step-by-Step Directions to Cook It:

1. Preheat the Ninja Foodi Digital Air Fryer Oven by selecting air fry mode
2. Add the onion and oil to the air fryer pan
3. Heat for 2 minutes
4. Add spinach, zucchini, and remaining ingredients
5. Cook for 15 minutes at 360°F
6. Cool for 5 minutes
7. Serve

Serving Suggestions: serve with orange juice

Preparation & Cooking Tips: slice the zucchinis

Nutritional value per serving: Calories: 131kcal, Fat: 6g, Carb: 4g, Proteins: 1.4g

Lemon with Potatoes Sauce

A stand out sauce among all. Lemon gives all meal a great feel, which makes this meal an excellent one

Preparation time: 10 minutes
Cooking time: 16 minutes
Serves: 4

Ingredients To Use:

- 1 tbsp of lemon zest
- 1 pound of gold potatoes
- 1/2 lemon juice
- Black pepper and salt
- 1 tbsp of chopped dill
- 2 tbsp of butter

Step-by-Step Directions to Cook It:

1. Preheat the Ninja Foodi Digital Air Fryer Oven by selecting air fry mode
2. Add the butter, potato to the air fyer oven pan and heat for 5 minutes
3. Add the lemon zest and the remaining ingredients
4. Cook for 11 minutes at 390°F
5. Serve

Serving Suggestions: serve with any juice

Preparation & Cooking Tips: grate the lemon zest

Nutritional value per serving: Calories: 123kcal, Fat: 4g, Carb: 4g, Proteins: 3g

Carrot with Lemon Leek

This combination produces a delightful meal. Follow the below recipe and have the best dinner.

Preparation time: 10 minutes
Cooking time: 16 minutes
Serves: 5

Ingredients To Use:

- 1 tsp of garlic powder
- 1/2 tsp of balsamic vinegar
- 2 leeks
- 2 tbsp of olive oil
- 1/2 cup of chicken stock
- 2 tbsp of lemon juice
- 1 tsp of ginger powder
- Black pepper and salt
- 1 tsp of garlic powder

Step-by-Step Directions to Cook It:

1. Preheat the Ninja Foodi Digital Air Fryer Oven by selecting air fry mode
2. Add the carrots, leeks, and the remaining ingredients to the Ninja Foodi Air Fryer Oven pan
3. Cook for 16 minutes at 380°F
4. Cool for 5 minutes
5. Serve

Serving Suggestions: serve with pineapple juice

Preparation & Cooking Tips: slice the carrots

Nutritional value per serving: Calories: 134kcal, Fat: 4g, Carb: 5.5g, Proteins: 2.6g

Apple with Radish

This is an excellent appetizer. It is a nutritious appetizer and contains a lot of vitamins needed for the body.

Preparation time: 10 minutes
Cooking time: 16 minutes
Serves: 5

Ingredients To Use:

- 1 lime juice
- 1 pound of radishes
- 1/4 cup of chicken stock
- 1 tbsp of cilantro
- 3 tbsp of tomato paste
- 2 apples
- Cooking spray
- 2 spring onions

Step-by-Step Directions to Cook It:

1. Preheat the Ninja Foodi Digital Air Fryer Oven by selecting air fry mode
2. Put all the ingredients in the Ninja Foodi Air Fryer Oven pan
3. Cook for 16 minutes at 360°F
4. Cool for 5 minutes
5. Serve immediately

Serving Suggestions: serve with juice

Preparation & Cooking Tips: chop the onion and cilantro

Nutritional value per serving: Calories: 123kcal, Fat: 6g, Carb: 5g, Proteins: 4g

Endives and Balsamic Cabbage

This is a great and delicious recipe. It can be made for a special occasion or family gathering

Preparation time: 10 minutes
Cooking time: 16 minutes
Serves: 3

Ingredients To Use:

- 1 tbsp of olive oil
- 1 green cabbage
- 2 shallots
- 1 tbsp of balsamic vinegar
- 2 endives
- 1/2 cup of chicken stock
- 1 tbsp of sweet paprika
- Black pepper and salt

Step-by-Step Directions to Cook It:

1. Preheat the Ninja Foodi Digital Air Fryer Oven by selecting air fry mod
2. Add the oil, shallot to the air fryer oven pan and heat for 2 minutes
3. Add the remaining ingredients
4. Cook for about 14 minutes at 360°F
5. Serve immediately

Serving Suggestions: serve with any juice

Preparation & Cooking Tips: chop the shallot and shred the cabbage

Nutritional value per serving: Calories: 121kcal, Fat: 3g, Carb: 4g, Proteins: 5g

Chapter 9: Soup, Stews, and Broths

Nut Soup

Nut soup is a unique recipe, perfect for dinner meal.

Preparation time: 16 minutes
Cooking time: 26 minutes
Serves: 5

Ingredients To Use:

- 2 cups of water
- 4 tsp of coconut oil
- 1 cup of cashew nut
- 1 cup of pecans
- 2 tbsp of stevia

Step-by-Step Directions to Cook It:

1. Preheat the Ninja Foodi Digital Air Fryer Oven by selecting air fry mode
2. Place the pecans and cashew nut in the food processor and pulse.
3. Add the cashew mix to the Ninja Foodi Air Fryer Oven pan
4. Add coconut oil, stevia, and water
5. Cook for 15 minutes at 360°F
6. Serve

Serving Suggestions: serve with a soup bowl

Preparation & Cooking Tips: cut the pecans in half

Nutritional value per serving: Calories: 261kcal, Fat: 23g, Carb: 13g, Proteins: 6g

White Cream Soup

This is a nutritious soup; it provides the body with so much energy. It is a great winter food and a healthy recipe.

Preparation time: 5 minutes
Cooking time: 18 minutes
Serves: 3

Ingredients To Use:

- 1 tsp of onion powder
- 3 ounces of mushrooms
- 2 cups of beef broth
- 2 ounces of short noodles
- 1/2 pounds of stew meat
- Pepper and salt
- 1-1/2 tbsp. of Worcestershire sauce
- 1/4 cup of sour cream
- 1/2 tsp of Italian seasoning
- 1 tsp of garlic powder

Step-by-Step Directions to Cook It:

1. Preheat the Ninja Foodi Digital Air Fryer Oven by selecting air fry mode
2. Add the sour cream, Worcestershire, mushroom, and garlic powder to the Ninja Foodi Air Fryer Oven pan
3. Add Italian seasoning, meat, onion powder, broth, pepper, and salt.
4. Cook at 360°F for 12 minutes
5. Add noodles and cook for 5 minutes
6. Serve immediately

Serving Suggestions: serve with beer

Preparation & Cooking Tips: blanch the noodles

Nutritional value per serving: Calories: 600kcal, Fat: 21g, Carb: 66g, Proteins: 41g

Garbanzo with Sweet Potato soup

After having a long day, this is the kind of soup to recover your strength. It is a good dinner recipe.

Preparation time: 5 minutes
Cooking time: 11 minutes
Serves: 3

Ingredients To Use:

- 1/2 tsp of ground cumin
- 1/2 yellow onion
- 1/2 tsp of ground cinnamon
- 1/2 pound of sweet potatoes
- 2 cups of vegetable broth
- Pepper and salt
- 1/2 tsp of ground ginger
- 1/2 tbsp. of garlic
- 2 cups of spinach
- 1/2 tsp of ground coriander
- 1 can of garbanzo beans

Step-by-Step Directions to Cook It:

1. Preheat the Ninja Foodi Digital Air Fryer Oven by selecting air fry mode
2. Put all the ingredients except the spinach into the Ninja Foodi Air Fryer Oven pan
3. Cook for 10 minutes at 360°F
4. Add spinach
5. Stir until spinach wilts
6. Serve immediately

Serving Suggestions: Serve with mashed potatoes

Preparation & Cooking Tips: Tear the spinach

Nutritional value per serving: Calories: 166kcal, Fat: 2g, Carb: 33g, Proteins: 7g

Black Bean and Chili-Quinoa Soup

This is a delicious soup. It can be eaten during cold weather when it is hot. It is a delicacy you should try.

Preparation time: 5 minutes
Cooking time: 21 minutes
Serves: 2

Ingredients To Use:

- 1-1/3 cups of vegetable broth
- 1/2 diced bell pepper
- 2 cups of vegetable broth
- 1 clove of garlic
- 1/3 can of black beans
- 1/2 diced onion
- 1 celery stalk

- 2 tbsp of quinoa
- 1 tbsp of tomato paste
- Salt
- 1/3 cup of diced tomatoes
- 1 medium of sweet potatoes
- 1 tsp of paprika with cumin

Step-by-Step Directions to Cook It:

1. Preheat the Ninja Foodi Digital Air Fryer Oven by selecting air fry mode
2. Put all the ingredients into air fryer pan
3. Cook for about 20 minutes at 360°F
4. Serve immediately

Serving Suggestions: Serve with mashed potatoes

Preparation & Cooking Tips: rinse the black beans and drain

Nutritional value per serving: Calories: 380kcal, Fat: 1.3g, Carb: 75g, Proteins: 19g

Cauli-Squash Chowder Soup

This soup is delicious, easy to cook, and timely. Follow the recipe below and have a wonderful meal.

Preparation time: 6 minutes
Cooking time: 13 minutes
Serves: 3

Ingredients To Use:

- 1 cup of vegetable broth
- 1 clove of garlic
- 1/4 cup of half and half
- 1 tbsp of oil
- 1/2 pound frozen cauliflower
- 1/2 tsp of dried thyme
- 1/2 diced onion
- 1/2 pound of frozen butternut squash
- Pepper and salt
- 1/2 tsp of paprika

Step-by-Step Directions to Cook It:

1. Preheat the Ninja Foodi Digital Air Fryer Oven by selecting air fry mode
2. Add the oil, garlic, and onion into the air fryer pan and sauté
3. Add the remaining ingredients
4. Cook for 10 minutes at 360°F
5. Put the mixture in a blender and pulse well
6. Serve immediately

Serving Suggestions: serve with cheese

Preparation & Cooking Tips: add pepper and salt to taste

Nutritional value per serving: Calories: 105kcal, Fat: 4g, Carb: 16g, Proteins: 2.3g

Creamy Coconut Soup

Coconut soup is a good recipe for spring. It is a sweet and healthy meal

Preparation time: 5 minutes
Cooking time: 10 minutes
Serves: 4

Ingredients To Use:

- 1 tsp of honey
- 1 clove of garlic
- 2 cups of chicken broth
- 1 can of pumpkin puree
- Black pepper and salt
- 1/2 chopped onion medium
- 1/2 cup of coconut milk
- 1/2 tsp of cayenne pepper
- 1/2 cup of plain yogurt

Step-by-Step Directions to Cook It:

1. Preheat the Ninja Foodi Digital Air Fryer Oven by selecting air fry mode
2. Mix all the ingredients in a bowl
3. Transfer the mix to the Ninja Foodi Air Fryer Oven pan
4. Set the timer to 10 minutes on a 360°F
5. Cook for 10 minutes
6. Serve immediately

Serving Suggestions: Serve with croutons on top

Preparation & Cooking Tips: chop the cayenne pepper

Nutritional value per serving: Calories: 185kcal, Fat: 11g, Carb: 23g, Proteins: 6g

Butternut Soup

This soup has great taste, and it is suitable for dinner. The recipe below is a special one.

Preparation time: 10 minutes
Cooking time: 20 minutes
Serves: 4

Ingredients To Use:

- 1 tsp of cinnamon
- 2 cups of winter squash
- 4 cups of chicken broth
- 1/2 cup of light cream
- 1/2 cup of diced carrots
- 1 tbsp of olive oil
- 1/2 cup of chopped celery
- 1/2 tsp of coriander
- Black pepper and salt
- 1 cup of diced onion

Step-by-Step Directions to Cook It:

1. Preheat the Ninja Foodi Digital Air Fryer Oven by selecting air fry mode
2. Put all the ingredients in the air fryer pan
3. Spray with olive oil
4. Set the Ninja Foodi Air fryer Oven to at Bake
5. Cover
6. Cook for 20 minutes at a 360°F
7. Serve immediately

Serving Suggestions: Serve in a soup bowl

Preparation & Cooking Tips: cut the winter squash into cubes

Nutritional value per serving: Calories: 46kcal, Fat: 0.5g, Carb: 13g, Proteins: 2g

Tomato Soup

Tomato soup is a nutritious soup. It has a lot of vitamins that work perfectly for the body. It is a good soup for winter

Preparation time: 10 minutes
Cooking time: 20 minutes
Serves: 6

Ingredients To Use:

- 3 tbsp of fresh basil
- 1 medium of onion
- Black pepper and salt
- 3 cloves of garlic
- 1 tsp of thyme
- 1 tbsp of olive oil
- 1/2 tsp of sugar
- 2 tbsp of balsamic vinegar
- 5 cups of fresh tomatoes
- 1/2 cup of heavy cream
- 1/2 tsp of cayenne pepper
- 3 cups of chicken broth
- 5 cups of fresh tomatoes

Step-by-Step Directions to Cook It:

1. Preheat the Ninja Foodi Digital Air Fryer Oven by selecting air fry mode
2. Add the olive oil, garlic, and onion to the pan
3. Sauté for about 4 minutes
4. Add the remaining ingredients
5. Cook for 15 minutes at 360°F
6. Serve immediately

Serving Suggestions: Serve in a star bowl

Preparation & Cooking Tips: add salt and pepper to taste

Nutritional value per serving: Calories: 158kcal, Fat: 2g, Carb: 33g, Proteins: 4g

Potato Soup

This is a perfect soup for the summer; it tastes delicious and is energizing.

Preparation time: 10 minutes
Cooking time: 26 minutes
Serves: 4

Ingredients To Use:

- 1-1/2 cups of heavy cream
- 2 leeks
- Black pepper and salt
- 6 medium of potatoes
- 2 stalks of celery
- 1 tsp of dried thyme
- 2 cups of chicken broth
- 1 tbsp of olive oil

Step-by-Step Directions to Cook It:

1. Preheat the Ninja Foodi Digital Air Fryer Oven by selecting air fry mode
2. Boil the potatoes and water in Ninja Foodi Air Fryer Oven pan for about 20 minutes at 360°F
3. Add the remaining ingredients
4. Sauté for about 6 minutes
5. Serve immediately

Serving Suggestions: serve with croutons

Preparation & Cooking Tips: peel and cube the potatoes

Nutritional value per serving: Calories: 165kcal, Fat: 5.3g, Carb: 26g, Proteins: 6.2g

Creamy Broccoli Soup

Broccoli is an excellent green vegetable for soup. It gives the body so much strength needed. It is a delicious soup

Preparation time: 10 minutes
Cooking time: 15 minutes
Serves: 4

Ingredients To Use:

- 1 head of cauliflower
- 1 medium of yellow onion
- 3 cups of broccoli floret
- 1 tbsp of olive oil
- 2 cups of almond milk
- 3 cloves of garlic
- Black pepper and salt
- 2 cups of chicken broth

Step-by-Step Directions to Cook It:

1. Preheat the Ninja Foodi Digital Air Fryer Oven by selecting air fry mode
2. Add the oil, garlic, and onion into the Ninja Foodi Air Fryer Oven pan
3. Sauté for about 3 minutes
4. Add the remaining ingredients
5. Cook for 12 minutes at 360°F
6. Serve immediately

Serving Suggestions: Serve in a soup bowl

Preparation & Cooking Tips: add pepper and salt to taste

Nutritional value per serving: Calories: 105kcal, Fat: 6g, Carb: 8g, Proteins: 4g

Chapter 10: Beans and Egg Recipes

Lisa's Black Beans

You can decide to cook these beans immediately or store them in the refrigerator for 2-3 days before cooking. This is a lovely and delightful meal.

Preparation time: 10 minutes
Cooking time: 2 hours
Serves: 4

Ingredients To Use:

- 3 tsbp of ground cumin
- 2 cups of dried black beans
- 2 tbsp of salt
- 2 tbsp of ground coriander

Step-by-Step Directions to Cook It:

1. Preheat the Ninja Foodi Digital Air Fryer Oven by selecting Bake mode
2. Add the beans, salt, coriander, and cumin to the Ninja Foodi Air Fryer Oven pan
3. Cook for 2 hours at 360°F
4. Allow cooling to make the bean liquid thick
5. Serve immediately

Serving Suggestions: Serve in a star-shaped bowl

Preparation & Cooking Tips: rinse the beans before cooking

Nutritional value per serving: Calories: 11kcal, Fat: 1g, Carb: 19g, Proteins: 8g

Basil and White Beans

This is a perfect meal for lunch. It is very tasteful and deserves a try.

Preparation time: 10 minutes
Cooking time: 30 minutes
Serves: 4

Ingredients To Use:

- 1-1/2 cup of white beans
- 1/2 tsp of granulated garlic
- 2 tbsp of chopped basil
- 1 tsp of lemon juice
- Pepper and salt
- 1/2 tsp of lemon zest

Step-by-Step Directions to Cook It:

1. Preheat the Ninja Foodi Digital Air Fryer Oven by selecting bake mode
2. Add all the ingredients to the Ninja Foodi Air Fryer Oven pan
3. Set the timer to 20 minutes at 360°F
4. Allow to cool for 5 minutes
5. Serve immediately

Serving Suggestions: serve with cream cheese

Preparation & Cooking Tips: rinse the white beans

Nutritional value per serving: Calories: 41kcal, Fat: 0.5g, Carb: 4g, Proteins: 8g

Black Bean Pepita Dip

Black bean dip is an excellent meal with high carbohydrate content. It is a perfect and tasteful meal.

Preparation time: 10 minutes
Cooking time: 30 minutes
Serves: 4

Ingredients To Use:

- 1/4 tsp of ground cumin
- 2 tbsp of chopped green chilies
- 1 lime juice
- 1/2 cups of black beans
- 1/2 cup of salted pepitas
- 1/4 tsp of spicy pepper
- 1/4 cup of water
- 1/4 tsp of lime zest
- 1/4 tsp of cayenne

Step-by-Step Directions to Cook It:

1. Preheat the Ninja Foodi Digital Air Fryer Oven by selecting bake mode
2. Add all the ingredients to the Ninja Foodi Air Fryer Oven pan
3. Cook for 30 minutes at a 360°F
4. Serve immediately

Serving Suggestions: serve with croutons

Preparation & Cooking Tips: rinse the beans well

Nutritional value per serving: Calories: 150kcal, Fat: 5g, Carb: 9g, Proteins: 18g

Smoky White Beans

This meal has a rich taste and softening feel. It is easy to make. It is a meal for any time of the day.

Preparation time: 10 minutes
Cooking time: 30 minutes
Serves: 6

Ingredients To Use:

- 1/2 tsp of apple cider vinegar
- 3 cups of white beans
- 1/4 tsp of mustard powder
- 1/2 cup of raw cashew
- 1/2 cup of nutritional yeast
- 1 tsp of smoked paprika
- 1 tsp of liquid smoke
- 1/2 cup of water
- 1 tsp of smoked salt

Step-by-Step Directions to Cook It:

1. Preheat the Ninja Foodi Digital Air Fryer Oven by selecting bake mode
2. Add all the ingredients to the Ninja Foodi Air Fryer Oven pan
3. Cook for 30 minutes at 360°F
4. Serve immediately

Serving Suggestions: serve with a veggie burger

Preparation & Cooking Tips: rinse the white beans well

Nutritional value per serving: Calories: 250kcal, Fat: 0.2g, Carb: 11g, Proteins: 36g

Cashew-Beans Queso

Cashew beans queso is a unique recipe. It is amazing. It is a perfect meal for dinner

Preparation time: 10 minutes
Cooking time: 30 minutes
Serves: 5

Ingredients To Use:

- 1 tsp of smoked paprika
- 1/4 cup of nutritional yeast
- 1–1/2 cups of white beans
- 1/2cup of nondairy milk
- 1 tsp of salt
- 1/2 cup of raw cashew
- 2 tbsp of green chiles
- 1 tsp of chili powder

Step-by-Step Directions to Cook It:

1. Preheat the Ninja Foodi Digital Air Fryer Oven by selecting air fry mode
2. Mix all the ingredients in the Ninja Foodi Air Fryer Oven pan
3. Cook for 30 minutes at 360°F
4. Serve immediately

Serving Suggestions: serve with nondairy milk

Preparation & Cooking Tips: alubia white bean is also an excellent bean to use

Nutritional value per serving: Calories: 90kcal, Fat: 4g, Carb: 11g, Proteins: 5g

Cheesy Egg Soup

A combination of egg and cheese make a delicious recipe. Making it in soup form is a unique recipe.

Preparation time: 10 minutes
Cooking time: 10 minutes
Serves: 4

Ingredients To Use:

- 3 tbsp of parmesan cheese
- 1/2 tsp of salt
- 2 tsp of spring onion
- 2 eggs
- 5 cups of chicken stock
- 1/4 tsp of black pepper
- 2 ounces of egg noodles

Step-by-Step Directions to Cook It:

1. Preheat the Ninja Foodi Digital Air Fryer Oven by selecting air fry mode
2. Mix the salt, chicken stock, eggs, and ½ cup of chicken stock in a bowl.
3. Pour egg noodle and the rest of the stock in the Ninja Foodi Air Fryer Oven pan
4. Cook for 2 minutes at 360°F
5. Transfer to a bowl
6. Pour the egg mix into the Ninja Foodi Air Fryer Oven pan
7. Cook for 4 minutes
8. Serve immediately

Serving Suggestions: serve with juice

Preparation & Cooking Tips: add salt to taste

Nutritional value per serving: Calories: 302kcal, Fat: 7g, Carb: 27g, Proteins: 33g

Egg Drop Soup

An egg soup has different ways of making it. It is a great meal that is preferable for breakfast

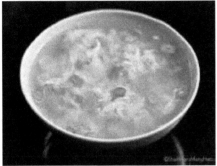

Preparation time: 10 minutes
Cooking time: 1o minutes
Serves: 2

Ingredients To Use:

- 4 medium quartered tomatoes
- 1 medium of sliced onion
- 1 egg
- 1 tbsp of cooking oil
- 2 liters of chicken stock

Step-by-Step Directions to Cook It:

1. Preheat the Ninja Foodi Digital Air Fryer Oven by selecting bake mode
2. Add the oil and onion to the Ninja Foodi Air Fryer Oven pan
3. Add the chicken stock and tomatoes
4. Set the Ninja Foodi Air Fryer Oven to sauté
5. Cook for 5 minutes at 360°F
6. Add egg and simmer for 3 minutes
7. Serve immediately

Serving Suggestions: serve with juice

Preparation & Cooking Tips: peel the onion

Nutritional value per serving: Calories: 30kcal, Fat: 0.8g, Carb: 5g, Proteins: 2g

Egg Puffs

Egg puff is a unique summer recipe; it is an excellent meal for breakfast. It is also a perfect meal for winter.

Preparation time: 10 minutes
Cooking time: 5 minutes
Serves: 4

Ingredients To Use:

- 1/2 tsp of baking powder
- 3 eggs, separate whites, and yolks
- 1/2 tsp of salt
- 1 tbsp of all-purpose flour
- 1 tsp of dried oregano
- 1/4 tsp of chili powder
- Cooking spray

Step-by-Step Directions to Cook It:

1. Preheat the Ninja Foodi Digital Air Fryer Oven by selecting air fry mode
2. Whisk the egg yolk in a bowl
3. Gently add a little amount of the yolk to the egg whites
4. Add salt, chili powder, oregano, flour, and baking powder
5. Spray oil on the Ninja Foodi Air Fryer Oven pan
6. Set the cooker to 350⁰F
7. Scoop the mixture into the oil
8. Cook for 2 minutes on each side
9. Serve puffs immediately

Serving Suggestions: serve with juice

Preparation & Cooking Tips: ensure you whisk the egg yolk well

Nutritional value per serving: Calories: 141kcal, Fat: 10g, Carb: 11g, Proteins: 6g

Sardine and Egg D'oeuvre

A combination of egg and sardine gives a tasteful meal. You can never go wrong with this recipe.

Preparation time: 10 minutes
Cooking time: 5 minutes
Serves: 4

Ingredients To Use:

- 1 tbsp of fresh parsley
- 3 eggs
- 1/4 tsp of white pepper
- 5 ounces of canned sardines
- 1/2 tsp of salt
- 1 tbsp of lemon juice
- 4 tbsp of mayonnaise
- Cooking spray

Step-by-Step Directions to Cook It:

1. Preheat the Ninja Foodi Digital Air Fryer Oven by selecting air fry mode
2. Mix all ingredients except mayonnaise in the Ninja Foodi Air Fryer Oven pan
3. Cook for 2 minutes on each side
4. Serve immediately

Serving Suggestions: serve with mayonnaise

Preparation & Cooking Tips: whisk the egg well

Nutritional value per serving: Calories: 468kcal, Fat: 19g, Carb: 37g, Proteins: 42g

Eggs, Onion, and Tomatoes

Tomatoes and onion give an egg a fantastic taste; it is a beautiful and delightful meal. It is a perfect meal for breakfast.

Preparation time: 10 minutes
Cooking time: 10 minutes
Serves: 2

Ingredients To Use:

- 1/4 tsp of dried basil
- 2 tbsp of olive oil
- 4 eggs
- 1 clove of garlic
- 2 tbsp of parmesan cheese
- 6 tomatoes sliced

- Cayenne pepper
- 1 small onion
- 2 big slices of crusty bread
- 1/2 tsp of salt
- 4 poached eggs

Step-by-Step Directions to Cook It:

1. Preheat the Ninja Foodi Digital Air Fryer Oven by selecting air fry mode
2. Add the oil, garlic, and onion to the Ninja Foodi Air Fryer Oven pan
3. Sauté for about 2 minutes
4. Add cayenne, cheese, tomatoes, basil, and salt.
5. Sauté for another 5 minutes
6. Top with poached eggs
7. Serve immediately

Serving Suggestions: serve with crusty bread

Preparation & Cooking Tips: use 4 slices of bread if it is smaller bread

Nutritional value per serving: Calories: 246kcal, Fat: 18g, Carb: 10g, Proteins: 14g

Chapter 11: Dessert and Snack Recipes

Tapioca Pudding

This is a perfect dessert for lunch; this recipe is an exceptional one. It is a special meal for summer.

Preparation time: 13 minutes
Cooking time: 30 minutes
Serves: 5

Ingredients To Use:

- 3 cups of whole milk
- 1/2 cup of granulated sugar
- 1 cup of tapioca pearls
- 1 tsp of vanilla extract
- 2 eggs
- 1/4 tsp of salt

Step-by-Step Directions to Cook It:

1. Preheat the Ninja Foodi Digital Air Fryer Oven by selecting bake mode
2. Add the milk, tapioca, and salt to the Ninja Foodi Air Fryer Oven pan
3. Cook for 5 minutes 360°F
4. Beat egg in a bowl and add 2 tbsp of tapioca
5. Add sugar and vanilla
6. Add the mixture to milk mix on the Ninja Foodi Air Fryer Oven pan
7. Adjust the temperature to medium and cook for 8-10 minutes
8. Allow cooling before serving.

Serving Suggestions: Serve with milk

Preparation & Cooking Tips: ensure sugar is enough

Nutritional value per serving: Calories: 527kcal, Fat: 18.3g, Carb: 72.1g, Proteins: 21.4g

Yellow Cake Pineapple

It is making use of pineapple to make cake gives a delightful recipe. It is a meal for any time of the day.

Preparation time: 14 minutes
Cooking time: 40 minutes
Serves: 5

Ingredients To Use:

- 1 cup of pineapple slices
- 1/4 cup of brown sugar
- 2 tbsp of butter
- 1 box of yellow cake mixture

Step-by-Step Directions to Cook It:

1. Preheat the Ninja Foodi Digital Air Fryer Oven by selecting bake mode
2. Drizzle melted butter and brown sugar into a springform pan that fits the Ninja Foodi Air Fryer Oven
3. Pour the pineapple slices into the springform pan
4. Pour yellow cake mix into the pan and cover with aluminum foil
5. Bake for 18 minutes 360°F
6. Allow cooling before serving.

Serving Suggestions: help with any juice

Preparation & Cooking Tips: ensure the mixture is homogenous

Nutritional value per serving: Calories: 669kcal, Fat: 14.1g, Carb: 134.2g, Proteins: 7.2g

Raspberry Cheesecake

This is a tasty dessert. Raspberry is an unusual fruit that gives the cake an exceptional feel.

Preparation time: 20 minutes
Cooking time: 55 minutes
Serves: 5

Ingredients To Use:

- 1 cup of granulated sugar
- 16 ounces of cream cheese
- 2 tbsp of brown sugar
- 3 tbsp of maple syrup
- 12 graham of crackers
- 12 big raspberries
- 1 tsp of vanilla extract
- 1/2 cup of heavy cream
- 2 tsp of cinnamon powder
- 2 tbsp of melted butter
- 2 eggs

Step-by-Step Directions to Cook It:

1. Preheat the Ninja Foodi Digital Air Fryer Oven by selecting bake mode
2. Crush the graham crackers in a plastic bag
3. Put it in a bowl and add butter with sugar
4. Pour the mix into a springform pan that fits the Ninja Foodie Air Fryer Oven
5. Set to the temperature and timer to 350°F and 6 minutes, respectively
6. Pour granulated sugar and cream cheese into a mixer
7. Mix until smooth
8. Pour mixture over the crackers crust
9. Put aluminum foil over the cake

10. Cook for 25 minutes at 360°F
11. Allow cooling before serving

Serving Suggestions: serve with orange juice

Preparation & Cooking Tips: ensure the pressure lid press the cake

Nutritional value per serving: Calories: 680kcal, Fat: 49.6g, Carb: 52.5g, Proteins: 12.5g

Caramel Popcorn

Popcorn is a good snack for movie dates and family movie nights. This is a special popcorn recipe that you should try.

Preparation time: 11 minutes
Cooking time: 10 minutes
Serves: 5

Ingredients To Use:

- 3 tbsp of brown sugar
- 1 cup of sweet corn kernels
- 1/4 cup of whole milk
- 4 tbsp of butter

Step-by-Step Directions to Cook It:

1. Preheat the Ninja Foodi Digital Air Fryer Oven by selecting bake mode at 360°F
2. Melt the butter and corn kernels with the heat
3. Cook until all the corn pops
4. Transfer the popcorn to another bowl
5. Pour milk and brown sugar on the pan and sauté
6. Cook for about 4 minutes
7. Pour the sauce on the popcorn and coat
8. Serve immediately

Serving Suggestions: serve with orange juice

Preparation & Cooking Tips: allow all the corn to pop

Nutritional value per serving: Calories: 190kcal, Fat: 15.5g, Carb: 15.2g, Proteins: 4g

Apricot de Leche

This is a great recipe; the meal has a delicious and yummy taste. It is easy to cook.

Preparation time: 11 minutes
Cooking time:56 minutes
Serves: 5

Ingredients To Use:

- 5 apricots
- 2 cups of condensed milk, sweetened

Step-by-Step Directions to Cook It:

1. Preheat the Ninja Foodi Digital Air Fryer Oven by selecting bake mode
2. Divide milk into 5 medium ramekins
3. Place the ramekins in it on the Ninja Foodi Air Fryer Oven pan
4. bake for 25 minutes at 360°F
5. Transfer the ramekins to a bowl
6. Allow cooling before serving
7. Serve with apricots

Serving Suggestions: serve with any juice

Preparation & Cooking Tips: set the temperature appropriately before cooking

Nutritional value per serving: Calories: 110kcal, Fat: 5g, Carb: 15.3g, Proteins: 5.2g

Blackberry Cobbler

Blackberry gives the meal a fantastic feel; you can never go wrong with it. This is a delicious recipe.

Preparation time: 14 minutes
Cooking time: 16 minutes
Serves: 4

Ingredients To Use:

- 1 tsp of vanilla extract
- 4 cups of fresh blackberries
- 1/2 tsp of cinnamon powder
- 1 tsp of vanilla extract
- 1/2 tsp of baking powder
- 1/2 & 1/4 cup of brown sugar
- 1/4 cup of water
- 1/4 tsp of nutmeg powder
- 3 tbsp of melted butter
- 1-1/2 tsp of salt
- 2 tbsp & 3/4 cup of plain flour
- 1/2 tsp of baking powder

Step-by-Step Directions to Cook It:

1. Preheat the Ninja Foodi Digital Air Fryer Oven by selecting bake mode
2. Mix 2 tbsp of flour, 1/2 tsp of salt, 1/2 cup of brown sugar, cinnamon, blackberries, vanilla, water, and nutmeg in a big ramekin
3. Put the ramekin on the Ninja FOodi Air fryer Oven pan
4. Cook for about 3 minutes at 360°F
5. Mix baking powder, flour, butter, salt, butter, brown sugar, and baking soda in another bowl
6. Pour the mixture on the blackberry mix on the air fryer oven pan
7. Cook for about 12 minutes at 325⁰F.
8. Allow to cool before serving

Serving Suggestions: serve with juice

Preparation & Cooking Tips: ensure you set the right temperature

Nutritional value per serving: Calories: 650kcal, Fat: 10g, Carb: 135g, Proteins: 10g

Mango Rice Pudding

Mango is a sweet and nutritious fruit; mango rice is a delicious and outstanding recipe. It is an excellent meal for a special gathering.

Preparation time: 11 minutes
Cooking time: 16 minutes
Serves: 5

Ingredients To Use:

- 1 tsp of vanilla extract
- 1 cup of jasmine rice
- Salt
- 2 cups of whole milk
- 1 mango
- 1/2 tsp of nutmeg powder
- 1 tbsp of unsalted butter
- 1/3 cup of granulated sugar

Step-by-Step Directions to Cook It:

1. Preheat the Ninja Foodi Digital Air Fryer Oven by selecting bake mode for 5 minutes
2. Mix the vanilla, rice, salt, milk, mango, nutmeg, sugar and add to the air fryer oven pan
3. Cook for 5 minutes at 360°F
4. Serve immediately or allow cooling before serving

Serving Suggestions: serve with cream cheese

Preparation & Cooking Tips: ensure the pressure lid covers well

Nutritional value per serving: Calories: 283kcal, Fat: 46g, Carb: 13g, Proteins: 9g

Baked Stuffed Apple

Baked apples give a distinctive taste; this recipe is an exquisite one. Fellow the recipe below, and have a great meal.

Preparation time: 16 minutes
Cooking time: 6 minutes
Serves: 5

Ingredients To Use:

- 2 tbsp of brown sugar
- 1/3 cups of chopped dates
- 1/3 cups of raisins
- 4 tbsp of chocolate sauce
- 1/3 cup of toasted pecan
- 1 tbsp of cinnamon powder
- 6 red apples
- 4 tbsp of butter

Step-by-Step Directions to Cook It:

1. Preheat the Ninja Foodi Air Fryer Oven to bake for 5 minutes at 325^{0}F.
2. Mix dates, butter, pecans, cinnamon, raisins, and brown sugar in a bowl
3. Stuff the mixture in apples
4. Arrange the stuffed apple on the air fryer oven pan
5. Cook for about 5 minutes at 325^{0}F.
6. Serve the stuffed apple with chocolate sauce topping

Serving Suggestions: serve with beer

Preparation & Cooking Tips: chop the pecans

Nutritional value per serving: Calories: 356kcal, Fat: 18g, Carb: 54g, Proteins: 3g

Cookie Pizza

Pizza is one of the best snack or appetizer you can have. Cookie pizza is a recipe you cannot recover from the sweetness.

Preparation time: 11 minutes
Cooking time: 36 minutes
Serves: 5

Ingredients To Use:

- 1 tsp of vanilla extract
- 22 ounces of sugar cookie dough, premade
- 1 package of cream cheese
- 5 tbsp of unsalted butter
- 2 cups of confectioner' sugar

Step-by-Step Directions to Cook It:

1. Set the Ninja Foodi Air Fryer Oven to bake and preheat for 5 minutes at 325°F.
2. Put the cookie dough on the air fryer oven pan.
3. Cook for 35 minutes at the same temperature
4. Put the cookie in the fridge to cool
5. Mix the cream cheese, vanilla, butter, and confectioners' sugar in a bowl
6. Serve cooled cookie with cream cheese spread on it

Serving Suggestions: top with any fruit like berries, pineapple, or mango

Preparation & Cooking Tips: set the appropriate baking temperature

Nutritional value per serving: Calories: 790kcal, Fat: 45g, Carb: 93g, Proteins: 8g

Salty and Sweet Bars

Bars can be in a different recipe. Sweet and salty bars are an excellent dessert for dates or family gathering

Preparation time: 6 minutes
Cooking time: 11 minutes
Serves: 11

Ingredients To Use:

- 1 bag of mini marshmallows
- 1 cup of light corn syrup
- 1 bag of potato chips
- 1 pack of candy-coated chocolates
- 1 cup of granulated sugar
- 1 cup of peanut butter
- 1 cup of crushed pretzels
- 1 tsp of vanilla extract

Step-by-Step Directions to Cook It:

1. Set the Ninja Foodi Air Fryer Oven to air fry mode and preheat for 5 minutes
2. Mix the sugar, vanilla, corn syrup, and transfer to the air fryer oven pan
3. Add peanut butter and marshmallows and until the marshmallows melts
4. Add pretzels and potato chips
5. Stir until pretzels and potato chips are well coated in marshmallow mix
6. Pour in a pan and serve in square

Serving Suggestions: serve with chocolate candies

Preparation & Cooking Tips: stir until all the mixtures are homogenous

Nutritional value per serving: Calories: 586kcal, Fat: 22g, Carb: 97g, Proteins: 10g

Conclusion

Many users love and appreciate the Ninja Foodi Digital Air fry Oven's speed, capacity, and multi-functionality. The wonderful flip away feature is the deciding factor for some and the topping on the cake for most.

Now that you know what a gem the equipment is, get a unit if you haven't already and join us on this incredible cooking adventure.

Good luck!

CPSIA information can be obtained
at www.ICGtesting.com
Printed in the USA
LVHW100841290321
682810LV00028B/485